MAYNARD CONCISE HISTORY OF EPPING FOREST 1860

EDITED BY

RICHARD MORRIS, OBE
Verderer of Epping Forest

WITH A LIFE OF JOHN MAYNARD BY

STAN NEWENS

LOUGHTON
LOUGHTON AND DISTRICT HISTORICAL SOCIETY
2005

ISBN 1905–2690–13

First published in 1860 by John Maynard
Reprinted in 1994
This completely reset edition published in 2005 by
Loughton and District Historical Society
and available from Forest Villa, Staples Road
Loughton, Essex
IG10 1HP

Design and typesetting by Ted Martin

Cover illustration
The Grimston Oak
from an old postcard

Printed in Great Britain by
Riverside Press Ltd
Ipswich

Contents

Editor's Preface

John Maynard wrote his history of Epping Forest at a time when the problems faced by the Forest were at their height, owing to the Crown's decision in 1805 to sell its forestal rights, and the subsequent enclosure by the Lords of the Manors of much of the 'waste' in their manors.

Maynard did not have the benefit of many of the records and documents unearthed by the Epping Forest Commission of 1871, which spent four years researching the history of the Forest. This possibly led him to give a slightly one-sided view of the Forest's history in the eighteenth and early nineteenth centuries. In 1854 George Palmer had addressed a pamphlet to 'The Freeholders in the County of Essex and those interested in the Forest of Waltham', drawing attention to encroachments on the Forest which were to the detriment of the 'Poorer Foresters', but Maynard was the first person to write a more detailed historical survey of the issues involved. They shared similar views and were vociferous during the same period in the nineteenth century. Although they came from different backgrounds, I am sure they must have known each other, or at least heard of the other's activities.

Maynard makes the occasional confusion between the three levels of forest courts, but this does not affect the story of their gradual decline, as the interest of the Crown in a 'royal forest for the pleasure of the monarch to hunt in', waned and had ceased by the end of the eighteenth century.

The reset text has been left unaltered except where minor factual errors have been corrected by the addition of a correct name or source, for instance, 'White's *History of Essex*', published in 1836, should refer to 'Wright's'; and similarly 'Hogborn's' is, of course, 'Ogborne's'.

John Maynard's contribution to recording the history of Epping Forest and Waltham Abbey needs to be acknowledged and a note on his life, written by Stan Newens, has been included.

Loughton, November 2005   RICHARD MORRIS*

*Author of *The Verderers and Courts of Waltham Forest in the County of Essex 1250–2000*, published by the LDHS in 2004.

The Life of John Maynard 1802–1871

John Maynard was a member of a well-known Waltham Abbey family. His great-grandparents, John and Mary Maynard, lived at Lingfield in Surrey but their son, Daniel, a shoemaker, moved from Sevenoaks to Cheshunt at the suggestion of the Upton family, who also became prominent in Waltham Abbey. Daniel's son, William Maynard (father of the author), was born in Cheshunt in 1799 but as a young man lived in London, Deptford and Gravesend. He married Elizabeth Woodbridge 1779–1852, descended from a long-established Waltham Abbey family, however, and established himself in business in the town as a stationer, toy dealer, bookseller and umbrella maker.

William and Elizabeth eventually had four sons and seven daughters and by the time of William's death at the age of 90 in 1869, there were said to be 80 children and grandchildren and upwards of 50 great-grandchildren.

John Maynard the author was born on 19 July 1802 at City Road, Finsbury, and his birth was recorded at the Eagle Street Baptist Church in Holborn, where his parents were worshippers. No information is available about his education, but he became a shoemaker and earned his living as such until his late thirties.

He married Mary Field at St Botolph's Church, Bishopsgate, on 3 April 1822 and they had at least six children: John, James, David Daniel, Eleanor, Emma and Thomas.

John and Mary lived in Waltham Abbey – at Broomstick Hill and later at Romeland – and two of their children, John and David, were admitted to the Leverton School.

Mary Maynard must have died at some time after the birth of Thomas, for on 28 November 1828, John Maynard, a widower, married Mary Ann Champness of Waltham Abbey at St Botolph's Church, Bishopsgate.

A change of career followed, perhaps through an interest developing into a profession.

The 1841 Census reveals that John and his second wife and the two youngest children, Emma and Thomas, were by then living at Epping Common [*sic*]. John, who was a musician, gave his occupation as an organ tuner. White's *Directory of Essex* 1848 lists John and Maria [*sic*] Maynard as teachers at the Workhouse School in Epping. Mary Ann Maynard, however, seems to have accepted a post as teacher at Theydon Bois National School in 1849.

The 1851 Census lists John as a schoolmaster at Lindsey Street, Epping, and Mary Ann, with his daughter, Emma, a teacher at School House, Theydon Bois. In 1861, according to the Census, John, described as an organ tuner, and Mary Ann, as a teacher, were both at School House, Theydon Bois, along with John's daughter, Emma. In the same year, Mary Ann was presented by Theydon Bois parishioners with a Bible as a token of esteem for her 'private and Christian character' and the 'kind, faithful, parental care' with which she had acted as Mistress of the School. The Bible is still treasured in the family to this day.

In 1871, they were still at Theydon Bois and Mary Ann was still teaching, but John's occupation was now given as a tax inspector. Unfortunately, he died at 69 years of age on 20 July 1871 and was buried in Theydon Bois Churchyard, although no gravestone or memorial survives there. He was described on his death certificate as a teacher of music.

Maynard's Concise History of Epping Forest was published in 1860 from the School House, Theydon Bois. In it, he gave not only a historical survey of the origins and development of the law and administration of the forest, but he also took up the case of the poorer inhabitants and defended their right to cut wood and pasture cattle. Although his version of the background has been overtaken by later research, his book is the first history of Epping Forest and the first counterblast in print against the arguments of those who wanted disafforestation and enclosure.

John Maynard later published a *History of Waltham Abbey* in 1865. Again, despite the earlier histories of the town by Thomas Fuller and J Farmer, his work was in many ways a pioneering venture. He claimed to have derived much information from an old manuscript book kept by the Pigbones family from which his maternal grandmother – Susannah Woodbridge 1741–1827 – was descended. Unfortunately no such manuscript book has survived or been mentioned by any other writer.

For one who could only have had a very rudimentary education and whose access to historical sources must have been very limited, the two publications represent a considerable achievement. He blazed a trail which others followed: in the case of Waltham Abbey the historian William Winters 1834–1893, who married his niece.

In addition to producing his historical works, John Maynard served as a teacher and was a good musician. He must have developed a great respect for learning, despite a humble background.

Of his descendants, much remains to be discovered. His son, John, is probably to be identified with an Epping bricklayer of that name. James Maynard became a shoemaker, married and had two children. David Daniel married Fanny Larter, daughter of a farmer, but died young. Thomas Maynard, the youngest surviving child married Jemima, became a cooper and moved out of the district. He was in Edmonton in 1861, according to the census of that year, and may later have moved to Lancashire.

John Maynard's daughter, Emma, married George Meagher at Theydon Bois in 1858 and had four children. One of his great-great-great-granddaughters via this descent is Rita Richardson, who lives in Norwich. She and another Maynard family descendant, Mrs Valerie Day of Nazeing, have played an important part in uncovering this story. Thanks are also due to Peter Huggins of Waltham Abbey Historical Society.

STAN NEWENS
President, Waltham Abbey Historical Society

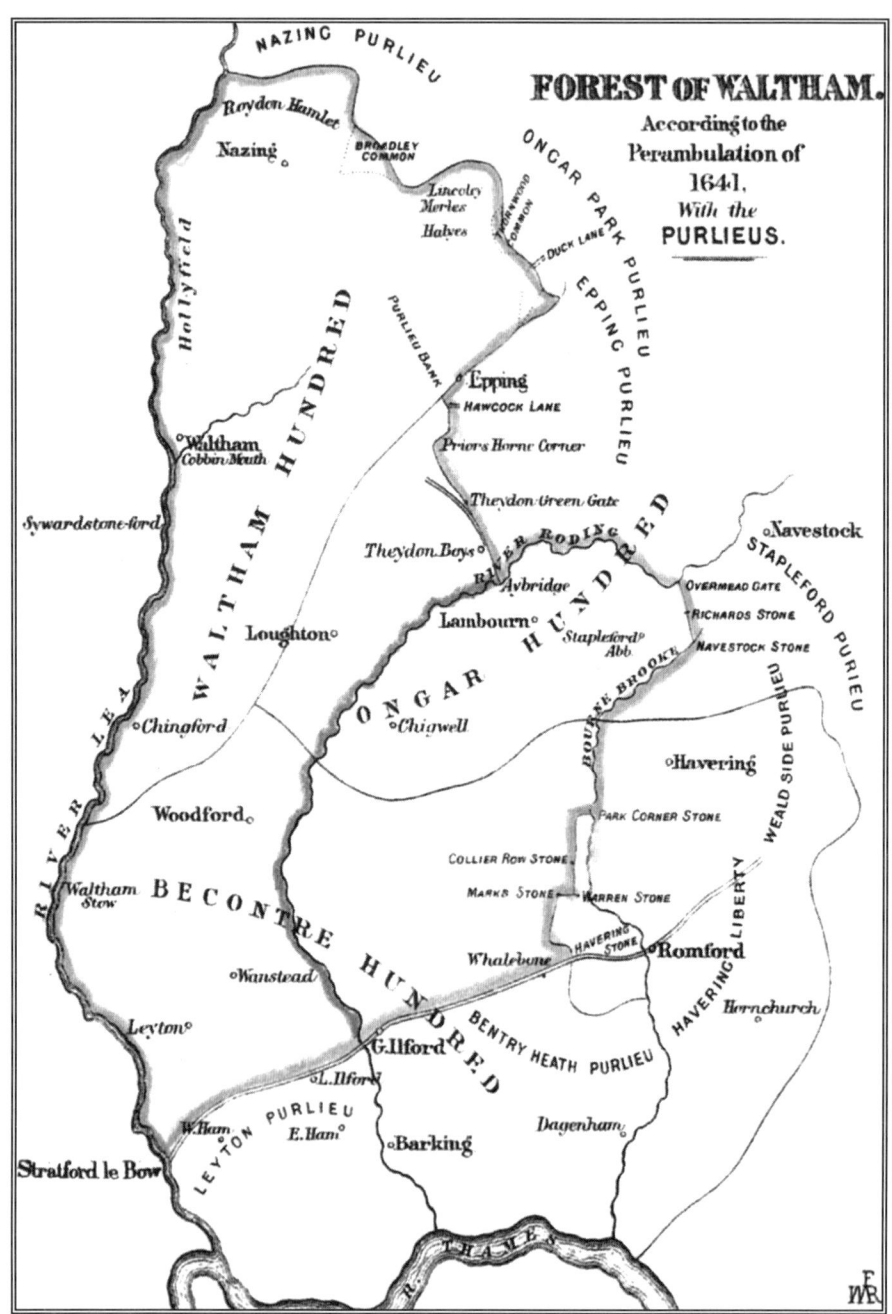

FOREST OF WALTHAM.
According to the
Perambulation of
1641,
With the
PURLIEUS.

viii

MAYNARD'S

CONCISE HISTORY OF EPPING FOREST

ITS ANTIQUITY, BOUNDARY, RIGHTS JUDICATURE, COURT, ETC

BRIEFLY CONSIDERED

WHEREIN

THE RIGHTS OF THE CROWN, THE RIGHTS OF THE PEOPLE, AND THE
RIGHTS OF THE LORDS OF THE MANOR ARE SHOWN

'Let me have men about me that are fat;
Sleek-headed men, and such as sleep o'nights;
Yon Cassius has a lean and hungry look;
He thinks too much; such men are dangerous.
            Would he were fatter;
            He reads much;
He is a great observer, and he looks
Quite through the deeds of men.' – SHAKESPEARE.

PUBLISHED BY THE AUTHOR

JOHN MAYNARD

SCHOOL HOUSE, THEYDON BOIS, ESSEX

1860

PREFACE

———————

In offering this compilation I merely observe that my aim has been to produce in one small work all the information to be obtained from authentic records relative to the forest affairs. I have studiously brought nothing forward which cannot be relied upon.

JOHN MAYNARD

1859

CONCISE HISTORY OF

EPPING FOREST

In studying this subject, it has occurred to the mind of the writer, with no small force of conviction, that in order to be able to treat of Forest matters, it will be necessary first to take a view of England when the greater part of it might have been called forest, and was entirely under our ancient kings and their nobles; there being, at that time, no middle class of society who had the least voice or influence in the framing of the laws whereby they were to be governed; so that in fact, at that time, there was no such thing as the laws of the people; but the laws of the king and the nobles were forced upon the people, who were slaves, and the property of the lords of the soil whereon they were born, and were generally conveyed with the estate from one owner to another, and were obliged to obey these laws, or die the death.

At this time the chief diversion of the king and his nobles was hunting; and in order to secure this pleasure to themselves, the most severe and cruel laws were made, and the people taught to know that such and such were the laws of the king, and that the nobles were the enforcers of these laws.

Space precludes the saying much relative to the cruelty and injustice of these laws; suffice it, therefore, to say, that there were different degrees of punishment for killing, and even for disturbing, the game of the forest, whether in enclosed or unenclosed lands. The greater the personage, the smaller the punishment; and so on through the different grades of society until it reached the slave, whose punishment was death. In course of time this punishment was changed from that of death to the putting out of the eyes. Whether this was done in order to mitigate the punishment, or to preserve their lives, in order that they might be seen helplessly crawling about, as a warning to others, I leave to the charitable, for them to pass their own opinion.

Dreadful indeed, must have been the times, when the life of a deer on the forest was more valued than the life of a fellow man.

There are still extant forest laws of this kind, attributed to King Canute, and also for the appointing of forest officers.

Thus we derive an impartial view of our now comparatively happy country as it was more than eight hundred years ago.

As our aim is to take an historical survey of Epping Forest, we shall confine our attention more immediately to the affairs of this remaining portion of the ancient forest of Essex, which at one time extended over the greater portion of the whole county, but which has been greatly reduced by our ancient kings' own enclosures, and by their grants to their favourites to enclose large portions as their own private estates, together with the disafforesting of whole districts at a time. One large portion, in the hundred of Tendring, was disafforested in the reign of King Stephen, and that part on the north side of the road leading from Stortford to Colchester was disafforested in the reign of King John. This took place after the barons obtained Magna Charta from him on June 17th, 1215, wherein some few clauses were introduced for the ameliorating of the forest laws, the necessity of which King John himself had taught; he having, in the ninth year of his reign, by his prerogative, caused the fences to be thrown down near the royal forests, and forbidden all hunting. This he did that his deer might have access to the cornfields, to spite his nobles and other of his subjects who had shown him that they were dissatisfied and opposed to his despotic and overbearing rule.

Much more of the county was disafforested in the reign of King Edward the First, and the boundaries of Epping, or Waltham Forest, were determined by a perambulation and inquisition held at Stratford Langthorn, by commission under the great seal of England, in the seventeenth year of the reign of King Charles the First, a copy of which will be found in the Appendix.

As it may not be uninteresting, we here introduce a copy of one of the charters of Edward the Confessor, written in verse, wherein he grants to Peperking the office of Grand Forester of his forest of Chelmer and Dancing, in the county of Essex.

> 'Ic Edward Koning
> Have yeven of my forest the keeping,
> Of the hundred of Chelmer and Dancing,
> To Randolf, Peperking, and his kindling,
> Wyth heose and hynde, doe and bock,
> Hare and foxe, cat and brocke,
> Wylde fowel with his flock,
> Partrich, fesant hen and fesant cock,
> Wyth green and wylde stob and stock,

1

To keepen and to yemen by all her might,
Both by day and eke by night.
And hounds for to hold
Good and swift, and bold;
Four greyhounds and six raeches
For hare and foxe and wylde cattes
And therefor iche made him my broke.
Witness the bishop Wolston
And brooke ylerd many on,
And Swein of Essex our brother
And taken him many other,
And our steward Howelin
That by sought me for him.'

There are two copies of this Charter: one taken from the Records of Hill. Term, 17th of Edward II, by Peter Le Neve; and the other from the Forest Rolls of Essex.

Salmon, in his *Antiquities of Essex*, says: 'These differ something in the writing, but the sense is much the same'; and he accounts for the slight difference, as probably arising from the copier being unable correctly to make out the letters or the words in the original, and so failing in making the one to be a perfect copy of the other.

We are informed by Wever that the copy of a Charter, in verse, granted by William the Conqueror, was found in the register-office of Gloucester, and is as follows:

'I William Kyng, the thurd year of my reign
Give to the Paulyn Roydon, Hope and Hopetown,
With all the bounds both up and down
From heven to yerth, from yerth to hel,
For thee and thine there to dwell
As truly as this kyng right is myn
For a crossbow and an arrow
When I sal com to hunt on yarrow
And in teken that this thing is sooth
I bite the whyt wax with my tooth
Before Meg, Maud, and Margery,
And my thurd sonne Herry.'

These two copies will be sufficient to show how our ancient kings used to act relative to forest matters; and also to show that they looked upon all the forests as their own; and wherein no person was allowed the privilege of hunting without the permission of the king.

Edward the Confessor built a palace at Havering, enclosing one thousand acres of forest-land, as a park for his palace.

5

Henry III, in the year 1250, granted leave to John de Lexington to enclose the park, known by the name of Hill Hall, in Theydon Mount; and in 1253 leave was granted to him to hunt in the forest of Essex.

Permission was also granted by the same king to Ralph Gernon to enclose the estate called Park Hall, in Theydon Garnon (otherwise Cooper Sale).

Space forbids further enlarging in detailed instances; and considering this to be sufficient, we proceed to take a retrospective view, and to follow up the hereditary line of the wardenship of the forest of Essex, through the reigns of the kings from the time of King Stephen until the giving up or the dissolution of the Forest Court, so long known by the name of the Forty-day Court.

King Stephen granted the grand-forestership or wardenship of the forest of Essex, together with the keeping of the park at Havering, to the family of Ralph de Montfitchet, and their heirs; and King Henry II confirmed the same offices to Richard de Montfitchet, and his heirs, in like ample manner, as his ancestors had held the same of the king's predecessor.

Richard de Montfitchet son of the above Richard de Montfitchet joined himself with the barons against King John, and was deprived of his offices; but in the reign of King Henry III he was restored, both to the wardenship of the forest, and to the keeping of the park at Havering. He alienated these offices in the fifty-first year of the reign of Henry III to Thomas de Clare; to whom they were confirmed by a charter, dated May 14th in the same year; from him it descended to his son, Gilbert de Clare, in the fifteenth year of the reign of Edward I, and then to his brother, Richard de Clare, in the first year of Edward II. He was succeeded by his son, who died without issue in the fourteenth year of the same reign, and left his two aunts, Margaret (wife of Bartholomew de Baddlesmore), and Maud (wife of Robert de Wells), as his co-heiresses.

(About this time the forest of Essex had become so much reduced, that the portion still remaining as forest appears to have received the name of Epping or Waltham forest on that account.)

Eventually, in the third year of the reign of King Edward III, the wardenship of Epping forest became vested in Maud, Countess of Oxford. On her decease (about the fortieth year of the reign of Edward III) she was succeeded by Thomas de Vere, Earl of Oxford, in whose family it was retained, the heir of each warden succeeding in the wardenship through the reigns of Richard II, Henry IV, Henry V, Henry VI and until the fifteenth year of the reign of Edward IV; when John, Earl of Oxford, gave offence and was put under attainder, which continued for seventeen years, during which time he was expelled the wardenship of the forest. He remained under attainder during the time of the murder of Edward V, who, with his brother, the Duke of York, was smothered in the Tower of London; or, in other words, through the twelve remaining years of the reign of Edward IV, and through the reign of King Richard III. In the first year of the reign of King Henry VII, he was by Act of Parliament restored to the wardenship of the forest, &c.

In the twelfth year of his reign, King Henry VIII (as he preferred Epping Forest to any other forest in England for hunting) requested to be allowed by John, Earl of Oxford to appoint his own officers over this forest. The Earl of Oxford yielded up the wardenship of the forest into the hands of the king, for his Majesty's lifetime; but it was not restored to the Oxford family until the reign of King James; so that the Crown held the wardenship, and exercised absolute control over the affairs of this forest, throughout the reigns of Edward VI, Queen Mary, and Queen Elizabeth. Upon this affair being related to King James, in the beginning of his reign, he restored the wardenship of the forest, with all its former emoluments, to Edward de Vere, Earl of Oxford.

About fourteen years after this transaction, King James granted permission to Henry, Earl of Oxford, to build a gaol, and to appoint a gaoler at Stratford, for the custody of offenders in forest matters; and also granted that the forest warden should have right to claim certain tolls from carts, &c during fence-month passing through the forest, for the support of this gaol. (Pardon a digression, merely to notice, that this toll was collected, years after the gaol was pulled down, but not without considerable murmuring and opposition from the payers of the toll. At length several spirited men refused to pay the toll any longer: and after some litigation, they convinced the forest-warden that he had lost his charter through doing away with the gaol.) But to return.

Henry, Earl of Oxford, conveyed the wardenship of the forest to William, Earl of Exeter, in the latter part of the reign of King James. In the third year of the reign of King Charles I, William, Earl of Exeter, conveyed it to Robert, Earl of Lindsay, his heir, who conveyed it to Sir Richard Child, Baronet, from whom it lineally descended through the families of Tylney and Long.

Catherine, daughter of Sir James Tylney-Long, the heiress of the families of Tylney and Long, married William Wellesley Pole, Esq (the late Lord Mornington), who held the wardenship of Epping Forest, in right of his wife, until the Forest Court was dissolved.

The verderers of this forest were elected by the freeholders of Essex; no doubt, to watch over the affairs of the forest, and over the interests of those more immediately concerned in forest rights. Charles, Earl of Dorset, sold Copped Hall, in the year 1700, to Thomas Webster, Esq; his son and heir, Sir Thomas Webster, Baronet, was Sheriff of Essex in 1704, chosen member of Parliament for Colchester, 1705, and elected by the freeholders of Essex, verderer of the forest in 1717.

This may serve to show that the freeholders of Essex had power to elect the verderers of Epping Forest; and if a right to elect, also power to reject, if they had seen it necessary. They appear at this time to have been alive to their own duty, and also to the interest of all who were concerned in forest matters and in forest rights. But now all the authority of this ancient court has, through the supineness of its officers, together with that of the freeholders been suffered to dwindle into insignificance until the forest appears almost to have fallen as a prey to the hawks of the land.

In 1816, the four verderers were, Sir Eliab Harvey, KCB, of Rolls, near Chigwell; William Joseph Lock-Wood, Esq, of Dews Hall, Lambourn, near Abridge; John Conyers, Esq, of Copped Hall, Epping; and Montagu Burgoyne, Esq, of Mark Hall, Harlow. These were all elected by the freeholders of Essex. Whether there have been any verderers of Epping Forest elected by the freeholders since these four appears very doubtful. The late John Conyers, Esq, the son of the above named John Conyers, appears to have succeeded his father as verderer by courtesy; and it appears very probable, as the affairs of this court were so badly attended to of late years, that everything was out of order; the freeholders never exerted themselves in regard to their right of electing new verderers as the office became vacant, and so lost their voice and interest; and at last became slighted and wholly set at naught by the remaining members of the Forest Court.

THE FOREST COURT AS IT APPEARED ABOUT FORTY YEARS AGO

Grand Forest Warden, William Pole Tylney-Long, Esq, Wanstead House.
The Lieutenant, or Deputy Warden, Sir William Smyth, Bart, Hill Hall,
    Theydon Mount.
Riding Forester, John Rigg, Esq, Walthamstow.
Purlieu Ranger, William Mathew Raiks, Esq, Walthamstow.

The forest was divided into ten Walks; and ten Master Keepers appointed:

1st, *Layton and Wanstead Walk*, Charles Danvers, Esq, Wanstead.
2nd, *Walthamstow Walk*, George Bowls, Esq, Wanstead.
3rd, *Woodford Walk*, Sir Robert Wigram, Bart, Walthamstow House.
4th, *New Lodge Walk*, William Sotherby, Esq, High Beach, Waltham Abbey.
5th, *Chingford Walk*, Lydia Heathcot, Chingford.
6th, *Epping Walk*, John Conyers, Esq, Copped Hall, Epping.
7th, *Loughton Walk*, William Mellish, Esq, Bush Hill, Enfield.
8th, *Lambourn and Chigwell Walk*, Rutherford Abdy, Esq, Albins,
    Stapleford Abbots.
9th, *West Heynault Walk*, John Maitland, Esq, Woodford Hall.
10th, *East Heynault Walk*, Jeremiah Harmann, Esq, Snaresbrook.

It must be obvious to all who have given the least consideration to forest matters, that this court embodied all the authority, all the forest-rolls of Essex, and all the forest-laws in itself; and to which all parties interested in this forest could make their appeal with the certainty of meeting with a hearing, and of having justice done to their suit; and it is also obvious, that the shutting up of this highly-valued and respected court is, in fact, tantamount to the stealing away from all persons concerned in the forest-rights, both the law and the means of appealing to that law, which was embodied in that court, both for the protection of the rights of the Crown and the rights of the people. The right of the Crown was merely feed and protection for the deer; and the rights of the people, residing within the bounds of the forest, was feed

9

for their cows and horses, the same as on other commons, save that they were compelled to drive home their cattle in the fence-month, as this part of the soil had been, under forest regulations, claimed for the feed and protection of the king's deer, and was therefore under the forest laws and the jurisdiction of the Forest Court; and if any one had reason to complain of any overbearing conduct from the lord of any manor within the forest, in regard to forest matters, he had this court to appeal to; and also, if any lord of a manor within the forest had any request or special claim to make, this was the authority for him to apply to.

'At a Forest Court, held October 4th, 1670, before Aubney [Aubrey], Earl of Oxford, Chief Justice in Eyre of the Forests on this side the Trent, and steward of the forest of Essex, the claims of the lord of the manor of Waltham upon this forest, with other liberties, immunities, privileges, &c, was very ample and extensive, comprehending whatever seemed to have been granted to the abbey; and to this document all persons concerned may at any time refer.'

Copied from the 453rd page of the second volume of
White's [Wright's] History of Essex.

This is the way historians could write twenty years ago; but now they are compelled to write the mysterious fact, that as the Forest Court is now withheld from the people, they are cut off from the means of appeal, from the sight of the forest rolls, and from the old records of forest administration. Is not this tantamount to a public fraud, and a public injustice? – and such an one as was never before tolerated by the legislation of England?

At the Forest Court, held in 1670, before mentioned, most of the lords of manors in the forest made their separate claims. All of them claimed pasturage for their cattle, save in the fence-month; and several claimed common of estovers or liberty of cutting wood on the wastes. The writer verily believes that, if we could obtain a sight of the forest rolls, we should find that the inhabitants of Epping, Waltham Abbey, Loughton, and Theydon Bois, claimed right of estovers (or wood-cutting), the same as Sewardstone did.

'The inhabitants of Sewardstone claimed not only pasturage in all the wastes there the whole year, save in the fence-month, but liberty of cutting wood on the wastes sufficient for their firing, from All-Saints to St George's; to be drawn away each time on a sledge only, with two horses.'

White's [Wright's] History of Essex, vol. ii.

'Dame Elizabeth Boothby claimed, within the forest, the manor of Chingford Comitis, with all the liberties, emoluments, commons, wastes, fisheries, court and other immu-

10

nities, and privileges thereto belonging. Also, for herself and tenants, common of pasture in the wastes in the forest; and liberty to cut down pollard trees upon her manor; likewise hedge-bote; and to appoint a sworn woodward for her woods of Larks and Danhurst-hill.'

White's [Wright's] *History of Essex*, vol. ii.

Many instances of appeals to this court might be brought forward; but believing this to be sufficient to show the importance and authority of this Forest Court, we pass on to notice that it had power from an ancient date to grant small enclosures; but still the grants made by the court to enclose pieces of forest land have been comparatively few; and in the main the whole forest has been both protected and preserved by the influence of its court.

From the most ancient times forest matters appear to have been valued, as being of more importance than the affairs of a county, the great aim of our ancient kings and nobles being the protection of the game of the forest. Therefore nothing less than the greatest honour the king could bestow upon it was thought to be sufficient; and, consequently, one of the chief amongst the nobles was chosen to preside over the affairs of the forest; whereas the sheriff, although chosen (at that time) by the king to preside over the affairs of a county, was generally one of inferior rank.

That the kings should have appointed the sheriffs until the 28th of King Edward I is not surprising, when we consider how much of the king's property they were entrusted with. William the Conqueror, at his distribution of the English estates amongst his Norman generals, took care to reserve one-third of each county to himself, the sheriff of each county being accountable for the rents and profits thereof to the king. In the 28th year of the reign of King Edward I, he granted in parliament to the people 'to choose the sheriff in every shire, except where the sheriffalty [*sic*] is of the fee, if they list'.

In the ninth year of King Edward II, on account of the insufficiency of sheriffs, the king and parliament appointed the nomination at the Exchequer by his great officers, that 'no person shall be, unless he have sufficient in the county to answer the king and the people'. But the forest protection was another thing, and required to be supported by the greatest honour the king could confer upon it; and to the forest affairs having been placed in the hands of rich and honourable men, who were above the reach of mean bribery, may be attributed the almost entire forest as it was when first committed to their keeping.

11

And although they had power to grant leave for enclosing portions of forest land, and if they saw the plea of the lord of the manor, whereon the portion of land was situated, to be reasonable, they complied with his request, yet they never adopted this as a general rule; but when they made such a grant, they did so rather as an exception to their rule. And if any portion of the forest was enclosed without their permission, save little pieces of waste land on manors, their custom was to send their under keepers to knock down the fences and throw it out. Perhaps, of all the manors enclosing pieces of copyhold, Theydon Bois stands the most conspicuous, both in regard to number and size of the pieces enclosed; but these, although they did not escape the eye of the Forest Court without some little animadversion, nevertheless escaped their vigilance.

Application was made to the Forest Court by a former lord of the manor of Theydon Bois, some twenty years ago, to enclose a portion of ground whereon to build a house for the clergyman. Upon the representation of their being no house for the clergyman, who on that account could not live in the parish where he had the cure of souls committed to his charge, and that one would be built by means of Queen Anne's Bounty, together with subscriptions, if the court would kindly give a grant to enclose a suitable piece of ground for that purpose, the lord of the manor agreeing on his part to give his right in the ground, the benevolent court granted their permission, and the lord of the manor enclosed the same, but the house was not built until some time after the ground was enclosed; during which time the lord of the manor let it out as poor men's gardens, one rood to each, at the rent charge of six shillings per annum, with the understanding that they were to give up possession when called upon to do so, as the ground would be required to build the clergyman's house upon, so soon as the proper arrangements could be made.

On these conditions the men held the ground two or three years, and derived some considerable benefit from it, insomuch that they felt the loss of it much when they were called upon to give it up. This was observable to all; and some kind and benevolent persons suggested, that, if a piece of ground for the purpose of poor men's gardens could be obtained by a grant from the Forty-day Court, it would be a most desirable thing; but this was not entered into until several years had elapsed; during which time, the present lord of the manor made an appeal to the Forest Court, and obtained a grant to enclose a piece of forest ground on his manor to build a family residence upon, there being no place suitable for his family upon his manor. He obtained the grant to enclose fourteen or fifteen acres I cannot be certain which to build his house upon. He enclosed the land, and dug out the earth for the foundation to be laid, and planted a few shrubs; but he never built his house nor laid one brick! He not only enclosed all that was granted, but he set up marks to cause persons to believe that he had a right to enclose where he had set up his flags; but one of the under forest-keepers, of the name of Eliot, watched over this affair with so much vigilance that only the portion granted was enclosed. He, however, went so far as to forbid wood-cutting on the parts where he had put up his flags; but one man of the name of Deemer, being instructed by Mr Eliot, the keeper, to go and cut his wood there, as he was in the custom of cutting wood on that as well as on other parts, he did so, and that without any molestation from the lord of the manor, although he saw him both cut and cart it home many times; and without doubt Deemer would have been justified, at that time, by the Forest Court, if he had been driven to make his appeal to that court against the lord of the manor, as he, the lord of the manor, well knew.

If Deemer had been in the wrong, as well as others who followed his example, why did not the lord of the manor make his appeal to the Forest Court?

Some time ago, three or four poor labouring men commenced a law-suit with the lord of the manor, on account of his annoying them in their wood-cutting, and brought the matter to a trial at Chelmsford; but instead of appearing, they became frightened, and allowed the judgment to proceed by default. The lord of the manor proceeded against them for the law-costs, and threw them into prison, where they remained some months in the debtors' gaol. Since which, the lord of the manor has carried things with so high a hand, that one might be almost ready to suppose that he considered that this incident gave to him absolute power over the forest affairs of Theydon Bois manor.

If these poor, simple-minded men had made their appeal to the Forest, or, in other words, the Forty-day, Court, as it was most generally called, they would have done wisely, and would have maintained their chartered rights still in their own hands, which would have been better than suspending them; but unfortunately, they went to the civil law, which, in fact, had no right to dictate in forest affairs, or in this matter; and then, at the very time when their cause could have been heard, for them to absent themselves was stupidity in the very extreme. It must, however, be a gratification to the parish of Theydon Bois to be able to reflect (although they wished these poor men success) that their doings cannot be construed into an act of the parish.

The clergyman's house was built by means of subscription, together with Queen Anne's Bounty and the forest grant of the enclosure of the land, although there was, and still is, in the parish, a parsonage-house; but that had in the course of time, though King Henry VIII must not be blamed for this, become the property of the lord of the manor, and is still known by the name of Parsonage Farm.

At length, some persons thought that another piece of ground might be obtained from the Forest Court for poor men's gardens, if the lord of the manor would give his permission to an application being made to the court for a grant to enclose a portion for that purpose. He, with all the semblance of benevolence and generosity, undertook to perform the whole on behalf of the poor, and so nicely pleaded their cause at the Forty-day Court, that he obtained leave to enclose a suitable piece for that purpose; he, on his part, promising to give his right in the ground: but, as some considerable expense would attend the clearing and enclosing, he requested to be allowed to make a charge upon the ground until he should have received the amount which he should be obliged to lay out in the requisite clearing, &c.

All things settled, he agreed with Mr Barnerd, of Woodford, to clear the ground for the wood which was upon it. Mr Barnerd employed a charcoal-burner Thomas Smith, of Loughton to make charcoal of the wood as his (Barnerd's) men stubbed it up.

In this way, the ground 14 acres was cleared without one farthing expense; however, the planting of the hedge round it, together with the two gates, and the ploughing of the ground, formed a debt upon it. The lord of the manor who apparently had done so much for the poor, industrious men of Theydon Bois, now put such hindrances in their way by making rules, and by binding them down to restrictions, that they would not have anything to do with it upon such terms and the ground was unoccupied for some time. At length, Mr Hatherel, one of the under forest-keepers, was instructed by the Forty-day Court to wait upon the people of Theydon Bois, and inform them that if the poor men, for whom the grant was made, did not soon occupy the ground, he was authorised, and must very shortly, knock down the fence and throw it out by order of the court. The clergyman, the

Reverend Barton Lodge, called upon the poor men, and inquired of them their reason for not taking possession of the ground which was granted by the Forty-day Court for their own private gardens. He was told by the whole of them, that the lord of the manor had made such laws and restrictions that they felt themselves prevented, and could not take possession of it upon such terms. All of a sudden, these hindrances were removed, and the poor men induced to occupy the ground, which, if not taken possession of by them, and by them alone, on whose behalf it was granted, would soon have been irrevocably forfeited and again thrown out. The Rev Barton Lodge was the chief instrument in prevailing upon the men to take possession of the ground, through kindly advising them to be careful of their own interest, and telling them that it would be but little they would have to pay as of debt upon the ground, and, that paid, the ground would be, as it were, their own and their children's after them, so long as they lived within the bounds of the parish. (Pardon a digression, merely to observe that if the poor men would not have taken possession of this portion of forest land, the lord of the manor would not have been allowed to do so.)

This ground was laid out in plots of one rood, with a charge of 5s. annually upon each plot, which the poor men paid, as they supposed, toward the liquidation of the debt, the amount of which they never could ascertain. In this way matters went on more than ten years, during which time the poor men worked hard, and, by manuring the digging (the lord of the manor having forbidden the using of the plough upon that ground), they got it into a high state of cultivation, when, to their great surprise, they were told that the lord of the manor would not allow them to hold it any longer! But any one still wishing to occupy a piece of ground for his garden, might have a piece in a little field which the lord of the manor had bought of Mr Styles, if they pleased. The poor men, thinking themselves helplessly constrained to yield up their right of this, their forest gift, after all their hard labour spent upon it (into the hands of the lord of the manor, as he laid his claim to it), did so; and those who saw fit hired a plot in this little field (the which field Mr Styles, some time ago, enclosed off from the waste, by the permission of a former lord of the manor, and which now the present lord offered to let), at the yearly rental of 5s. for each plot of only 20 perches. The lord of the manor has now let this ground, which was granted by the Forest Court as a free gift to the poor, and which is known by the appropriate name of New Zealand, as arable land (where the plough may now be used, of course), together with three other pieces of forest land, lately added to it. Poor, poor men, and poor blind parish, to its own interest, thus tamely to submit to the law of the dogs; the larger dog stealing the bones from the little ones, without regard to honesty or the rights of any. 'Facts are stubborn things', but just and equitable dealing never yet rendered them disagreeable or reproachful to any one.

The method always adhered to by the Forest Court, was to knock down any fence which had been erected without the leave of that court. This is now a precedent for the people.

On a survey of Waltham or Epping Forest, it was computed to contain about 60,000 acres, 48,000 of which is enclosed, and 12,000 wood and waste unenclosed.

Heynault Forest, which was also called the King's Forest, contained upwards of 3,000 acres. It was part of the possessions of Barking Abbey, and at the dissolution of abbeys it became vested in the Crown, and so it remained until lately, when by Act of Parliament it was enclosed, disafforested, and sold; but the other parts of the forest are not affected by this Act, as they were not Crown land.

By the ancient forest laws the Crown had right to feed and protection for the deer, in the enclosed as well as in the unenclosed portions of the forest; which right it still claims, and now offers to sell to the lords of manors situate within the bounds of the forest, if they wish to purchase it, and thereby relieve their manors from any interference from the Crown officers relative to the Crown forest right, – but nothing more, for it has nothing more to sell.

It has been said that, by way of compensation for any injury the deer might do in the enclosed portions of the forest, the occupiers of the enclosed lands have right of common pasturage for their horses and cows on the forest, except in the fence-month, i.e., fifteen days before and fifteen days after old Midsummer day; but those who have taken into their consideration ancient affairs relative to the various portions of unenclosed lands in England, see that unenclosed lands were, from the most ancient times, common to all the residents who held enclosed lands within the vicinity of such unenclosed lands as were known as such and such commons; they, upon reflection, consider that, instead of the forest conferring a benefit upon persons possessed of enclosed lands within the forest, it has been a hindrance, by reason of annoyance from the deer, and the owners of those lands being obliged to fetch home their beasts from off the forest, and there keep them for thirty days; whereas no such thing would have affected them if this part had not been chosen for a forest, as it would have then been a free common wherein they would have been entitled to a portion, even under the Commons Enclosure Act.

The forest rolls show that the claims made to and admitted by the Forest Court are various, some manors claiming one privilege and some another.

The Forest Courts were formerly held at Chelmsford, where they appear to have been held before the disafforesting made in the time of King Stephen, at about 40 days between each; hence the name of the Forty-day Court. This court was, for convenience, removed to the King's Head, Chigwell, where it continued to be held (with the exception of one short interval, when it was held at the White Hart, Abridge), to suit the convenience of the lieutenant, Sir William Smijth, Bart, of Hill Hall, Theydon Mount, who was the deputy-warden; and William Joseph Lock-Wood, Esq, of Dews Hall, Lambourn, near Abridge, who often acted for the grand forest warden, in his absence; but it was soon found to be more convenient at the King's Head, and it was therefore again removed thither, where it remained until the Forest Court was discontinued; having occupied it, from soon after the time when King James granted to Henry, Earl of Oxford, permission to erect the gaol at Stratford for the custody of offenders in forest matters, being more than 260 years.

In the dwindling of this court its meetings became more and more irregular, and like its other affairs, but little attended to. This ancient, honourable, and highly valued court, may date its decline from the lamentable period when Wanstead House was pulled down.

The warden held the following rights: to venison throughout the forest; to the fallen deer; to the browse wood on the forest; to tolls collected at Stratford during the fence-month; and to other emoluments.

The lieutenant, the verderers, the riding-foresters, the purlieu ranger, the steward and each of the master-keepers, were entitled to venison.

The warden used to receive annually at the exchequer, out of the civil-list revenue, for the woodward and ten under-keepers, £20 each, and £10 each for the riding purlieu rangers.

The Royal Liberty of Havering was at one time very closely connected with the Forest Court, as may be seen from the rolls of the forest of Essex. 'The Pleas of the Forest of Essex shew Leave obtained, from the King I presume, for erecting a Chapel here.' (Salmon's *Hist. Essex*, p. 249.) Salmon is here speaking of Romford Chapel, dedicated to St Edward, in the time of King Edward III. This Royal Liberty of Havering was wholly under the control of the reigning sovereigns, who, in several instances, chose for their park-keeper the person who was at the same time warden of the forest, from which an error has arisen; and the hasty assertion has been made by some historians that the keeping of the park at Havering was always attached to the wardenship of the forest, which was the case only at times. Mr Vincent's collections from the Tower Rolls serves to prove this.

In the reign of King Henry II, William Hurel held lands, by the sergeancy of keeping the park at Havering.

Henry Fitz Archer was sergeant or keeper of this park and was commanded by King Henry III, in the seventh year of his reign, to allow one John, keeper (no doubt under-keeper) of the park at Havering, to have the tops of the timber trees there felled, in like sort as his ancestors were wont to have the same in the reign of King John. This appears to have been during the time when Richard de Montfitchet before mentioned was deprived of his offices through joining himself with the barons against King John, and before he was restored to them by King Henry III; or Henry Fitz Archer (who lies buried in Cooper Sale Church) might have filled both offices during the expulsion of Richard de Montfitchet. One of these Fitz Archers is, in 5 Edward II, in a fine, styled Ballivus Forest Regis de Waltham; but as Mr Vincent says, 'this could not mean the chief forestership, because that was in other hands'. The family of Clare then possessed the wardenship of the forest of Essex.

Edward II appointed one Gerund to the keeping of the park of Havering.

Edward III appointed, first Aumeny, and after him one Tyle, to the same office.

Richard II appointed one Lowike.

Henry V appointed, first Norbury, and after him Randell.

Henry VI appointed three keepers to Havering Park, first Skergill, second Kemp, and third Boyse.

Edward IV appointed Sir Thomas Montgomery both to the office of the wardenship of the forest, and to the keeping of the park at

Havering during the time when John, Earl of Oxford, was under attainder.

In the first year of the reign of King Henry VII these offices were restored to the Earl of Oxford by Act of Parliament; after which we hear no more of Sir Thomas Montgomery as forest warden &c. This same king Henry VII granted the custody of the palace at Havering to his secretary, John Kendal; so it does not appear that the custody of the palace went with the keeping of the park.

In an old account of extent and valuation of Havering many curious customs are mentioned, which serve to show the low state of agriculture at that time. We copy from it the names of some of the tenants, with their fines:

'Simon Weyland holds the Hogland, and pays per annum half a mark; because hogs are wanting.

The heir of William, the weaver, holds the shepherd land, and pays per annum 12s.; because cattle are wanting.

John le Messinger holds one ploughman's land, and pays per annum 12s.; because a plough is wanting.

Adam le Wardour holds the land of another ploughman, and pays per annum 12s.; because a plough is wanting.

William Anon holds the blacksmith's land, and pays per annum 5s.; because a plough is wanting.

Amount of fines of the aforesaid lands for the king's table, 47s. 8d.'

(See Ogborne's *History of Essex*.)

Henry III granted to William Fitz William of Havering, in fee, six score acres of land in Havering for the service of finding litter in the king's chamber, whenever the king and his heirs should come to Havering.(Cartae Antiquae, 19 Hen III, m. 3 in the Tower.) He also granted to Ralph Fitz Solomon, three half-pence per day for his wages, as keeper of the king's palace garden and park at Havering, to be paid to him in the same manner as he received the same, in the time of Henry, the king's grandfather, and with all the rights and customs which Solomon, the park-keeper, father of the said Ralph enjoyed. (Cartae Antiquae, 19 Hen III, in the Tower.)

This man, although called park-keeper, was only a servant, and at best more than bailiff and head gardener; whereas the head keeper of the park held it as an honour conferred upon him by his king. This view will enable us to account, in a great measure, for the discrepancy which we frequently meet with, in finding some writers speaking of one person being keeper of the park at Havering, and others speaking of another person as holding the same office, both at one date.

Queen Elizabeth several times occupied this palace. In 1578, Lord Burleigh, then attending on the queen, received a letter from the University of Cambridge, informing him (who at that time was their high chancellor) that they had a desire to present to Her Majesty a well-bound book; and requested his influence and advice, as they were desirous of an opportunity to discuss some moral topics in her presence. He replied to their letter, dating his reply from the court at Havering, July 15, 1578. The queen received the University at Audley End, July 26, the same year. For more particulars see Nichols's *Progresses of Queen Elizabeth*, vol. iii.

Queen Elizabeth appointed Sir Thomas Heneage (captain of her guard, treasurer of her chamber, vice-chamberlain of her household, chancellor of the Duchy of Lancaster, and one of her privy-counsellors) to the keeping of the park and palace at Havering.

Samuel Fox, son of John Fox the Martyrologist, was employed by Sir Thomas as his secretary, and under Sir Thomas became deputy-keeper; at which time the palace had fallen so much into dilapidation that in 1596 a survey of it was taken. The survey was written by Samuel Fox, and is now preserved in the British Museum.

In Queen Elizabeth's time, the wardenship had not been restored to the Oxford family, who had yielded it up to King Henry VIII for his lifetime; and the appointing of the forest-officers together with the appointing of the park and palace-keeping of Havering, remained in the Crown during the reigns of Edward VI, Queen Mary, and Queen Elizabeth; but King James restored the wardenship of the forest to the Oxford family in the beginning of his reign, as before noticed. In 1608, King James granted to Thomas Haynes, twopence per day and pasturage for twelve cows in Havering-park, and six loads of firewood yearly during life. (Record in the Audit Office.)

By an Act of Parliament in the time of Oliver Cromwell, the palace of Havering was pulled down and sold, as part of the possessions of Charles Stewart and Henrietta Maria, late king and Queen of England. Salmon informs us, in his *History of Essex*, 'the lands are still in the Crown, but leased out'.

When Queen Elizabeth took the reins of government, she very tenaciously clung to the whole of the regal authority and possessions over which her father had exercised the least control, and acted as she saw fit relative to forest matters. She might not have been aware how it happened that her father became possessed of the absolute control of Epping Forest, and, therefore, might have concluded that she, by his right, possessed the same; and surely, if former sovereigns had right to grant leave to enclose whole estates out of the forest land, such as Hill Hall with its park, and the estate known as Park Hall, &c, she possessed the right to bestow the privilege of cutting firewood upon any part of the forest, on any party or parish she pleased thus to favour.

This queen had a little house upon the forest, where she very often resided; part of which is still standing, near to Chingford, or rather nearer to Fair Mead Bottom, High Beach, in the parish of Waltham Abbey, and still bears the name of Queen Elizabeth's Lodge. She might have noticed the abject poverty of many around her lodge, and might have seen the poor things shivering about with cold, and at the same time, she might have noticed that there was an abundance of wood at hand, whilst it was at their peril to touch it. She might have reflected that they were then deprived of all the advantages and gifts which they, the poor used to receive from the abbey which, until its dissolution which happened in the reign of her father, had the care and the comfort of the poor committed to its officers, whose duty it was to relieve the afflicted and destitute poor, who now had lost all relief or help save that which they might obtain from individual benevolence, as all the interests for the relief of the poor were given to the wings of the wind, to be blown away (together with the revenues of the church) into the hands of the fortunate rich favourites of the court. These things might have crossed the mind of the penetrating Elizabeth. Be it as it may, it is impossible to gainsay the fact, that she granted the privileges of wood-cutting to the poor of these parishes contiguous to her lodge (i.e., Loughton, Theydon Bois, Waltham Abbey, and Epping, all of which formerly belonged to the Abbey of Waltham Holy Cross), upon the tenor of observing the rule which she gave them, and which they were to retain as their charter; which was, to strike the axe into the boughs of the trees at the midnight of the 11th of November in each year, so as to begin to cut the wood, as nearly as possible, between the 11th and 12th of that month only; after which they were to cut it and bring it home at their pleasure throughout the season.

This chartered right is now disputed by some persons who envy the poor this privilege, by pretending that they cut it by a mere prescription, and not by a granted royal charter; whereas the more the matter is examined, the more the fact of its having come into custom from having originated in a charter given by Queen Elizabeth will appear.

In the first place we notice that when these parishes were in the possession of the Abbey, the people had no such privilege, no, not the Abbey itself.

Again, the very situation of Queen Elizabeth's Lodge goes to prove that such a thing could not have taken place under the very eye of such a queen without her notice and sanction, as no such thing as a pre-scription had existed for the inhabitants of any parish to go bodily and cut firewood on the forest before her time.

Another strange and remarkable coincidence is, that each of these parishes should have commenced at one and the same time, and that, too, under so singular an arrangement; and such a one, that if these parishes could have invented it, they would, in all probability, not have agreed amongst themselves to have chosen one date, one time of night, and one method.

Some but these are generally interested persons have raised objections to this method; saying that such a thing was beneath the dignity of a sovereign to establish as a charter; and have therefore, either hastily or purposely, asserted, that this method was nothing more than a mere freak of the vulgar poor. But let them reflect upon the methods given or used by our ancient kings, and whereby their favoured ones held their manors and estates – such as the presentation of a red rose, a pair of gloves, &c, on a certain day; upon the tenure by which they held their estates; the omission of which would have for-feited these estates; – and surely this method given by Queen Elizabeth was not more strange, as a charter, than the watching of the ward-staff, whereby many of the estates near the Rothings of Essex were held.

Many estates were granted by charter without any writing; some-times by a cup, a knife, or a sword: 'Edward the Confessor gave the rangership of Brentwood [Berewood in Dorset] forest, with a hide of land, to one Nigel and his heirs, to be held by a horn.' (Hogborn's [Ogborne's] *History of Essex*, p. 164.)

William the Conqueror conveyed the lordship of Broke to the Priory of St Edmundsbury by supplicating the Saint, and laying on the altar a knife wrapped up, in the presence of his nobles. (Bloomfield's, *History of Norfolk*.)

What if Queen Elizabeth had given the privilege of wood-cutting to be held by the possession of a certain horn; all of these parishes could not have held it, and if it had been given to one to hold in behalf of the rest, that one might have lost it in some way, so that the others might have had no means of securing their charter and their right; or if any separate thing had been given to each, they might not have had where to keep it so that it should not have been stolen from them; or in time it might have been claimed as the personal privilege of those who held it, &c, &c; so that the more we consider this matter, the more we shall discover the penetrating genius and character of Queen Elizabeth, and see her wisdom in appointing this truly singular method for the poor of each of these parishes to observe as their charter.

It may not be improper to notice here, that the warden of the forest had command of the browse-wood of the entire forest, as one of his emoluments, when he yielded up the wardenship into the hands of King Henry VIII. But since its restoration the wardens (seeing that it was disposed of) have never made their claim upon these parts, where they found the right had been granted by Queen Elizabeth to the poor.

This right and privilege, in course of time, aroused the envy of some persons who were a step higher than the poor; Waltham Abbey first discovered those who, by cunning and artifice, succeeded in depriving the poor of this privilege by inducing the poor to partake of a general drunk [*sic*] and supper on the 11th of November, 1641, so that the people of Waltham Abbey held it only through the remaining portion of the reign of Elizabeth, and through the reign of King James to the sixteenth year of King Charles I. At this time all parties knew by what tenure the poor held this chartered privilege.

The supper, which was a snare, had the effect of causing the unsuspecting poor of Waltham Abbey to forget their charter and their forest wood-cutting rights. They were soon made sensible of their error, and were prevented from gathering up pieces of wood from off the forest by these very persons who kindly gave them so sumptuous a supper – given, as they were led to believe, in admiration of their good conduct, as they were flattered, and told that no other parish could boast of such praiseworthy and deserving poor as the parish of Waltham Abbey. But, alas! they found out the snare too late. This information the writer derived from an old manuscript book of the Pigbones (an ancient family of Waltham Abbey); the writer's grandmother, being of that family,

23

had it in her possession, and from it he copied the date and the facts of the case.

Although the poor were thus deceived, and lost their charter, still their right never reverted either to the forest-warden or to the Crown; but instead the wood was allotted into portions of different sizes, and appointed to each farm or house having land belonging to it. The larger the landholder, the larger his share of the wood on the forest. Thus they became possessors of the wood, the right of the poor, without either charter or prescription.

The same scheme was tried at Loughton, but without success; and although many accepted of the supper there given, one, an old man, gave the signal, when he with others at once proceeded to the forest and duly secured their charter.

The poor of Epping maintained their right until a period now almost within the memory of man, but they were most treacherously inveigled into giving their right of wood-cutting into the hands of the lord of the manor, who promised to protect their rights and interest, and to make it more advantageous to them, if they would allow him the favour of cutting the wood after his own plan, in order that the forest should not appear so unsightly as it then did. If they would allow him to cut it after his own plan, he would not only cut it ready for their use, but he would even cart it to their own homes, as all he desired (he begged to assure them) was to improve the general appearance of the forest. The people consented, and he kept his promise with them several years; he then made them pay for the carting of the wood, and at length refused to cut any more. Upon this the copyholders and cottagers waited upon him, and told him if he would not cut it they would; but he forbade them at their peril to touch one twig of the forest, for they had lost their charter and therewith their right; and he was now fully determined to prosecute any one whom he could catch in the act of cutting wood in the forest. This lord of the manor of Epping was the John Conyers, Esq, who was elected by the freeholders of Essex as one of the verderers of the forest.

Theydon Bois may not yet be so hopelessly lost, as they have not yet failed in the observance of the charter; but they have been for some time past prevented from going as formerly (through groundless fear of the usurping power of the lord of the manor) openly to fetch it home; and now, even poor women are ordered off the forest, and threatened with imprisonment, if found gathering up a few sticks;

24

while thousands of fagots are being carted off from this part of the forest by the lord of the manor.

There is need yet, in this highly favoured country, for disinterested and honest men to arise to the help of the poor against the power of the oppressor.

When the poor of Waltham Abbey lost their charter, the wood was allotted to the landholders, still reserving the feed for the cattle. Epping was not allotted; one swallowed the whole of the wood as his right, without either charter or prescription. Lucky man, to have been allowed to do so! However, it appears to have formed a precedent for others to do the same, if they can do away with the charter by prevailing with the people to give it up, no matter how vile the means used. Still this would in no way affect the commonable pasturage.

The lord of the manor of Theydon Bois has not only assumed to have absolute power over the forest-wood, but has enclosed large portions of the forest, whereby he has shut out the cattle from these parts, and has acted as though he, by purchasing the right of feed and protection for deer which is all the Crown had to sell, had obtained absolute right over all things on his manor. He may have purchased the Crown forest-right, but not the absolute right over the land, to take away the commonable feed for cattle; the which right the people had even so to speak before this land was made forest. True, [the] Government has enclosed Heynault forest; but not without a special Act of Parliament for that purpose. But where shall we find a precedent to allow the enclosure of commonable manors without either a charter granted by a king or an Act of Parliament, save in the manor of Theydon Bois or Woodford, where the lord of the manor has been taught by litigation that the people can claim sufficient pasturage for their cattle? Could such things have been attempted unless an hoodwinking had been first secured?

Here the writer deems it proper to notice that very strange and remarkable incident, namely, the real, or perhaps feigned, quarrel between the forest-warden and the forest writing clerk. The clerk, it is said, made a demand upon the warden for a very large amount of money, which he said was due to him from the warden for personal attendance, for court-writing and other things performed by him in his official capacity as clerk to the Forty-day Court. The warden refused to pay him, and the quarrel ended in the clerk taking away all the forest documents in retaliation on the warden; so that all these old and valuable writings, the property of the Crown and of the people, were, so to speak, stolen away, and all parties interested in forest matters were cut off from all means of appealing to the forest-rolls; and thus things relative to the forest and its court stood still and in uncertain suspense, for a considerable time.

While things were in this state, a commission under the Crown was appointed, which appeared to be regarded as a strange thing, as there had not been one since that held to ascertain the boundaries of this forest in the reign of King Charles I. Many persons thought that these commissioners would soon bring the forest-clerk to his senses, and cause him to restore the court-rolls, both of the ancient and of the modern forest of Essex; but no such thing was ever publicly heard of! If the clerk still has these old records in his possession (which I much question), I would advise him to use all endeavours to keep them in safety, as they will, every year, increase in value, if only for sale to the Antiquarian Society.

The sole business of the commissioners appeared to be an endeavour to ascertain what, and all, the knowledge the people had relative to forest matters, by causing them to each send in, on the day of their meeting at the Forty-day Court, held at the King's Head, Chigwell, answers to certain questions proposed in the schedules which each was to deliver into the commissioners' hands, wherein each person was to state his claim, and also upon what tenure he founded his claim.

After this court, things remained some considerable time as though all the forest affairs had fallen into sleepy suspense and dull uncertainty.

The next thing we are permitted to see or to know relative to forest affairs is, that some of the lords, whose manors were within the forest, had purchased the Crown right; and we see them endeavouring, by actions which speak louder than words, to make the people believe that they, by purchasing the Crown right, had, to all intents and purposes, obtained absolute right and full authority to enclose, to build, and to sell, and in fact, to do as they pleased with all the unenclosed lands on their respective manors; claiming the whole as their own private property, without regarding, in any way, the claims of such as those who, from time immemorial, had held the right of pasturage for their cattle on these parts; and all this merely because they had purchased the Crown forest-right, which I again loyally and soberly assert, was merely feed and protection for the deer belonging to the Crown,

26

and nothing more; for there is no Act of Parliament to authorise even the Crown, and much less the lords of manors, to take away the common pasturage from the persons holding lands within the boundaries of the forest; neither is there any Act of Parliament that will justify the enclosing of any manor to effect a robbery upon those who have a right of pasturage upon such manor.

The Woodford affair has shown very clearly, that although the lord of that manor had purchased the Crown right, and had, by that deed, obtained more authority to grant enclosure of waste pieces on his manor, he has, nevertheless, been taught, by litigation, that he must leave sufficient pasturage for the cattle; and that the idea of his right to enclose the whole as his own personal property because he has purchased the Crown right, is not only erroneous, but unreasonably unjust.

But the mystery of mysteries, and the crowning wonder of the whole affair, as regards forest matters, appears to be in allowing the forest writing-clerk to steal away from this ancient court of English judicature all its valuable records with impunity! Things relative to the forest-laws, to the rights of the Crown, to the rights of the people, to the rights of the freeholders to have their voice in forest matters as they used to have in the electing of the four verderers, to watch over the general affairs for the good of all who were interested in forest matters, together with the writings relative to the hereditary wardenship, the chartered right of the heir of an ancient and noble family, and the utter destruction of the court itself – all brought about (who would believe it ?) through a freak of the clerk of the court – through his taking away every record from the Crown, from the warden, and from the people, because he and the warden differ about the amount of money, – this appears to be very strange and unaccountable forest jumbling indeed. The warden must be a very patient man to bear all this, and not to plead, even with the Crown, that the hereditary rights of his heirs should be secured to them. His heirs are, indeed, to be pitied, if the naughty clerk has, by taking away the forest records, caused them to lose their ancient chartered honours, rights, and forest emoluments. And, moreover, this naughty forest-clerk ought to be well horse-whipped if he, by taking away the forest-rolls of Essex, has so much offended the nation as to cause it to refuse protection to hereditary interests any longer. Under all these circumstances, who can help admiring the willingness of the forest-warden to be happily submissive

27

under every trying and humbling stroke of that government who, like the poor warden himself, is obliged, no doubt, to submit to the loss of the forest rolls? The warden becoming such a loser, begins to be humble and prudent both at once; and in order to make this mysterious and unaccountable forest-bungling carry the appearance of honest straightforward business, he sets the example to be patient and to comply with all, come what will; and in setting this example he purchases the Crown right on his manors, and commences cutting, clearing, slashing, building, and enclosing, as though he, too, thought to make the public believe that he had, by purchasing the Crown right, secured to himself absolute right over all the land on his manors. 'Where ignorance is bliss, 'tis folly to be wise.'

How it could have happened that the lords of these manors could not have seen that their manors were really commons, although under the name of forest, is somewhat surprising; but the old adage still has meaning, for 'there are none so blind as those who will not see'. Covetousness often blinds our better sight; but if the lords of manors are so blind, and cannot see that the people have a claim upon all commons, even under the Common Enclosure Act, the people and the government of the country are not so blind. In regard to Heynault forest, where the land belongs to the Crown, government was not so blind to this right of the people, and, therefore, they made reserve of a sufficient and suitable portion of land for the pasturage of the cattle of that locality.

Lastly, when the commissioners appointed by the Crown held their meeting at the Forty-day Court, (in the schedules which each person was provided with) they admitted the people's commonable right by requiring them in these schedules to specify the value of their claims; and to say if they were willing to accept of terms as an equivalent. Why was all this, if the Crown had absolute right and the people none?

What, if the Crown has seen fit to sell its forest-right? – this act of theirs does not compel the people to drive off their cattle and give up possession to the lord of any manor, although he may have purchased the Crown forest right.

The parishes wholly within the bounds of the forest are Waltham Abbey, Nazing, Epping, Wanstead, Leyton, [Walthamstow], Woodford, Chingford, Loughton, Chigwell, Lambourn, and Stapleford Abbots.

Those partly in the forest are East Ham, West Ham, Little Ilford,

Barking, Dagenham, Navestock, Theydon Bois, and Roydon, all of which should now arouse themselves to their own interests and also that of their neighbours.

Appendix

A PERAMBULATION of Waltham or Epping Forest was made in the twentieth year of King James by all the officers of the Forest Court and their under-keepers; but as no account of this perambulation was formally sent in to Government, a commission was appointed in the seventeenth year of the reign of King Charles I to determine the boundary of this forest. The inquisition is as follows:

'Essex SS

An inquisition taken at Stratford Langthorn, in the county of Essex, on Wednesday, being the 8th day of September, in the seventeenth year of the reign of our Lord Charles, by the grace of God, of England, Scotland, France, and Ireland, King, Defender of the Faith, &c., before Thomas Bendish, Bart., Benjamin Ayloofe, Bart., William Roe, Knt., Henry Holcroft, Knt., William Martyn, Knt., Camaliel Copiell, Knt., James Altham, Esq., William Conyers, Esq., Thomas Fanshaw, Esq., Edward Keighley, Esq,, Carew Harvey *alias* Mildmay, Esq., and Edward Palmer, Esq., three of the verderers of the forest of the said lord the King, of Waltham, otherwise called the Forest of Essex, John Wright, Esq., and William Attwood, Commissioners of the same lord the King, by his letters patent under his Great Seal of England, bearing date at Westminster, the 16th day of August, in the above seventeenth year of the reign of the said lord the king, to them, among others, directed, to inquire and find, by the oaths of good and lawful men, and by the oaths of witnesses, to be produced at the aforesaid inquest, and by all other lawful means, all and singular the meers, metes, bounds, and limits of the forest aforesaid, that were commonly known to be the meers, metes, bounds, and limits of the said forest in the twentieth year of the reign of the late King James, of England, &c., according to the tenour of a certain Act published and provided in the present Parliament, now assembled at Westminster, in the county of Middlesex, entitled, an Act for the certainty of forest, and of the metes, meers, limits, and bounds of the forest, and to do and perform all and singular things that are concerning the inquest aforesaid to be taken and returned and for doing of those things which, according to the tenour of the said Act, are to be done and performed. By virtue of which commission the Commissioners aforesaid made a certain warrant, directed to the sheriff of the county of Essex aforesaid, to return before five of the Commissioners aforesaid, or one of them, at the day and place aforesaid, forty and eight good and lawful men of the county aforesaid, to inquire of and upon the premises specified in the same commission. At which day and place Richard Luckyn, Esq., then Sheriff of the county aforesaid, as well by virtue of the writ of the said lord the king of *venire facias*, directed to him in behalf, returned to the Commissioners aforesaid his writ and warrant aforesaid; and that he had caused to be summoned, according to the form and effect of the writ and warrant aforesaid, among others, Thomas Manwood, Gent., Peter Westcomb, Gent., John Sorel, Gent., John Levet, Gent., William Gray, Gent., Thomas Aylett, Gent., Francis Nicholson, Gent., George Thorowgood, Esq., Thomas Lake, Gent., Robert Bragge, Gent., Samuel Plumme, Gent., George Gittens, Gent., John Wright, Gent., William Lake, Gent., William Finch, Gent., Robert Dawges, Gent., Lang Rous, Gent., Edward Fulham, Gent., John Mead, Gent., George Sames, Gent., Samuel Freeborne, Gent., George Savel, Gent., Henry Smith, Gent., Edward Digby, Gent., and Edward Humfrey, Gent., good and lawful men of the county of Essex aforesaid; which Thomas Manwood, Peter Westcombe,' [and all the others before-named, and which I need not here write or name again,] 'being solemnly called, appeared, and in the presence of the Commissioners aforesaid, and of Thomas Cooke Esq., Steward of the Forest aforesaid, and of Richard Searl, William Stains, William Wylett, John Golding, Thomas Wynch, Richard Maynard, William Johnson, Ralph Baker, William Millington, Richard Huddon, and Nicholas Spackman, Regarders of the Forest aforesaid, [Under-keepers, which were then called Regarders] and also in the presence of John Betts, Richard Belch, William Wills, Gervase Knight, John Cox, Henry Bream, William Comes, Edward Hoy, and William Soydery, Under-foresters of the Forest aforesaid; the same Henry Bream, Under-ranger of the Liberty of Havering and Bower, and William Wills, Under-ranger of Epping and Woodford, Sewardstone and Woodridden Fee, in the county and forest aforesaid, and also George Floyd, Under-ranger of Leighton, and Edward Batty, Under-ranger of Westhenault, and John Knightriding, Under-forester of the whole forest aforesaid, assisting and attending on the execution of the same commission.

The jurors aforesaid were sworn and charged to inquire, and to find all and singular, the meers metes, bounds, and limits of the said Forest of Waltham, otherwise called the Forest of Essex, which were commonly known to have been the meers, metes, bounds, and limits of the same forest, in the aforesaid twentieth year of the reign of the same lord James, late King of England, &c., as aforesaid. Which jurors, as well by view upon their perambulation, as by the oaths of divers credible witnesses, produced at the inquest aforesaid, sworn in the presence of the same sworn Commissioners and of the officers of the forest aforesaid, say upon their oath, that all and singular the meers, metes, bounds, and limits of the said Forest of Waltham, otherwise of the Forest of Essex, in the county aforesaid, which are commonly known to have been the meers, metes, bounds, and limits of the same forest, in the aforesaid twentieth year of the reign of the said lord James, late King of England, &c., were, and in the same twentieth year, were commonly known to be as followeth, viz.:–The said meers, metes, bounds, and limits of the said forest began, on the same twentieth year, at Stratford Bridge, called Bow, under which runs the River Lee, and going to the hundred of Becontree, by the king's highway, to Great Ilford, and from Great Ilford directly by the same king's highway, leading toward Rumford, to a certain quadrivium (or way, leading four ways), called the four wants, where late was placed, and yet is, a certain side of a whale, called the Whalebone; at which quadrivium (or path, leading fourways) one way thereof leads on the south part towards Dagenham, and other way thereof on the north part thereof towards Collier Row, and so going straight from the quadrivium aforesaid to and upon the aforesaid king's highway, leading towards Rumford aforesaid, towards a certain lane called Bean's Lane; at the head or beginning of which lane a certain stone, or boundary-stone, is now set and erected, engraved, and named Havering Stone. And so going in the lane aforesaid, between certain lands, called Bean's-land, to the left hand, to a certain other land, called Twenty-acres (parcel of the demesne lands of the Manor of Marks), and so returning into the land aforesaid, between the aforesaid land called Bean's-land on the south, and the aforesaid other lands called Twenty-acres on the north, to and into the aforesaid way leading from the quadrivium aforesaid to the Collier Row aforesaid; and so going in the aforesaid way, leading, from the aforesaid quadrivium against Collier Row aforesaid, by and near the site of the mansion-house of the said Manor of Marks to a certain elm marked with a cross, growing at the right hand of the same way, where a certain gate now is leading from the aforesaid way into a certain warren, called Marks-warren; at which gate there is now set and erected a certain other stone, or boundary-stone, engraven, and called Mark's Stone; and from thence going to the warren aforesaid, directly eastward, by the bounds dividing the said parish of Dagenham from the liberty of Havering at Bower, to a certain corner in the same warren, where now is set and erected another stone, or boundary-stone, engraven, and called Warren Stone; and from thence by the aforesaid bounds, dividing the aforesaid parish of Dagenham from the liberty of Havering aforesaid to Collier Row aforesaid, to a certain place near the messuage called Capcious, where now is set and erected a certain other stone, or boundary-stone, engraven, and called Collier Row Stone; and from thence downward, by the said metes and bounds, dividing the parish of Dagenham aforesaid from the liberty of Havering at Bower aforesaid, to the west corner of the park of the said lord the king, called Havering Park; at which west corner, commonly called Havering Park Corner, a certain other stone, or boundary-stone, is now set and erected, engraven, and called Park Corner Stone; and from the aforesaid stone, or boundary-stone, called Park Corner Stone, the meers, metes, bounds and limits of the forest aforesaid do further extend themselves, and in the same twentieth year of the said late King James of England, &c., did extend themselves by the pales and sides of the park aforesaid, called Havering Park, to a certain current of water called or commonly known by the name Bourne Brook; and from thence going by the banks of the same brook to the house of one Robert Making, in the parish of Navestock, near which house a certain other stone or boundary-stone is now set and erected, engraven and called Navestock Stone; and from thence, on the right-hand turning, leaving the aforesaid house, by the hedge and side of a certain common called Navestock Common, directly to the gate called Richard's Gate, near to which gate, likewise, a certain other stone, or boundary-stone, is now set and erected, and called Richard's Stone; and from thence by a hedge of the land of the said Robert Making, leading directly to the gate called Overmead Gate, and from thence to the river Rodon; and from thence by the river aforesaid to Aybridge, otherwise called Assbridge, and passing over the bridge aforesaid by the king's highway straight to the parish church of Theydon Boys, and so going on by the king's highway aforesaid to the mansion-house of the rector of Theydon Boys, to the gate called Thoydon Green Gate, and thence by the hedge called Hedge-purlieu to a corner of a certain hedge called Piershorne Corner; and so by the hedge aforesaid called Purlieu Hedge to the end of a certain lane called Hawcock Lane; and so to the bank near the end of the town of Epping called Purlieu Bank; and so going by the bank aforesaid to a place called Bennet's Corner, according to the bounds, limits, and divisions of the parishes of Epping and Thoydon Garnon, including within the forest aforesaid all the parish of Epping lying within the bank aforesaid, and excluding out of the forest all the parish of Theydon Garnon; and so going by the bank aforesaid to the end of the lane called Duck Lane, and so to the corner of the great waste called Thornwood Common; and so going by the bank aforesaid called Purlieu Bank, lying near the hedge on the south part of the common aforesaid, to a certain current of water which runs down from a ditch lying under the hedge aforesaid and the aforesaid bank called Purlieu Bank near a certain elm, which is the sole limit and boundary between the parish of Epping aforesaid and Northweald Basset, and also between the two half hundreds of Harlow and Waltham, and further going by the current of water aforesaid to the ditch before and near the mansion-house of one William Spranger, situated upon the side of the waste and common of Thornwood aforesaid; and from thence returning by the ditch aforesaid, to the mansion-house of one Daniel Hudson, likewise situate on the side of the common aforesaid; and so by the metes and divisions dividing the aforesaid two half hundreds of Harlow and Waltham, to a certain free Hay, called Lynceley-gate, including within the forest aforesaid parcel of the waste or common called Thornwood Common, as it lies within the current of water aforesaid; and also including within the forest aforesaid, the aforesaid tenement of the said Daniel Hudson, and a certain small grove called Hale's Grove, and all and singular lands and tenements there lying in the said half hundred of Waltham; and so going to the gate called Lincely-gate, above a certain piece of land, called Lincely Marles, and straight from thence going over the river's banks called East-field-hedge to a place called Lyme Holes Corner; and so passing over the king's way leading to the Church of Epping unto Pynn-croft leading to a bridge, called Pynn-bridge, and so going from the bridge aforesaid called Pynn-bridge, by the hedge called Purlieu-hedge, to the gate called Cologgaet's-gate, striking into the king's highway leading to a place called Syviars Green; and so descending in the king's highway, called Kennet's Lane, straight to the waste or common called Bradley Common, compassing the hamlet of Roydon to the river Lee aforesaid; and from thence to the corner of the marsh, called Odymarsh; and so passing over the river Lee aforesaid, including within the forest all that marsh called Holy-field Marsh, to the meadow called the Fryth, and so passing the Fryth, at the place called the Shirelake, to a marsh, called Hook's Marsh, including within the forest aforesaid all those marshes called Hook's marsh and Normarsh; and so going by the river Lee, likewise including all that great marsh, called Waltham Great Marsh; and so over the ditch there to the bridge called Smal-Lee Bridge, extending to the side of the same bridge downward by the ditch or a current of water running to the right hand of the king's highway leading to Waltham Abbey as far as Cold Hall, and presently beyond Cold Hall turning by a ditch or current of water, that divides the counties of Essex and Hertford, to a river, there including within the forest aforesaid all that meadow or marsh called Canward's; and from thence to a certain place called Cobbingmouth; and from thence by the river of Lee aforesaid to a meadow called Spencer's Mead; and so going onward by the river aforesaid to Sewardstone Ford; and there passing the marsh, called Ware-marsh, to the ditch called Marditch; and so going onward by Marditch to the river Lee aforesaid, and from thence, by the river aforesaid, to Broadmead, in the parish of Walthamstow; and from thence by the river aforesaid, to the bridge called Lock Bridge, now broken down, where now for passage is used Trajetus a ferry and from thence by the same river of Lee to the fore-nominated bridge of Stratford Bow, commonly known by the name of Bow Bridge.

And the jurors aforesaid say further, upon their oaths aforesaid, that the forest, of the said lord the king, of Waltham, otherwise called the forest of the lord the king, in the county of Essex aforesaid, extended itself in the said twentieth year of the reign of the late King James of England, &c., as is before by the aforesaid meers, metes, bounds, and limits, divided and expressed, and no further. And that the aforesaid meers, metes, bounds, and limits of the forest aforesaid above-mentioned and expressed in the said twentieth year of the said King James of England, &c., were, and were vulgarly known and reputed the true and certain meers, metes, bounds, and limits within which the forest aforesaid had no other ampler or larger meers, metes, bounds, and limits of the forest aforesaid in the said twentieth year of the said late King James of England, &c., as could any way appear to the jurors aforesaid.

And the Jurors aforesaid further say, upon their oaths aforesaid, that in the hundred of Becontree aforesaid in the aforesaid twentieth year of the late King James of England, &c., there remained entirely within the forest the villages of Wanstead, Leighton, Walthamstow, and Woodford. And that the village of Stratford, West Ham, East Ham, Little Ilford, Great Ilford, Barking, and Dagenham, in the hundred of Becontree aforesaid, did then partly remain out of the forest aforesaid viz. all the lands, woods, and hereditaments of the same villages as they lie on the right-hand of the king's highway aforesaid leading from the bridge of Stratford-le-Bow aforesaid towards Rumford aforesaid, and partly then remained within the forest aforesaid, that is to say, all and singular lands, woods, and hereditaments of the villages aforesaid on the left-hand of the king's highway aforesaid, as they are above divided by metes and bounds; and that in the aforesaid twentieth year of the said lord, the late King James of England, &c., the Liberty of Havering of Bower, in the county aforesaid, and the park there, commonly called Havering-park, together with all other lands, tenements, woods, and hereditaments in Hornchurch, Rumford, and Havering, in the said county of Essex, and in other parishes and members, appendances to the said Liberty of Havering, remained entirely out of the forest aforesaid. And that in the same twentieth year of the said lord, late King James of England, &c., in the hundred of Ongar aforesaid, there remained the village of Lucton, otherwise Loughton, Chigwell, Lambourn, Stapleford Abbots; and the village of Navestock and Theydon Boys, in the aforesaid hundred of Ongar, remained partly within the forest aforesaid, and partly out of the forest aforesaid, as they are above more at large divided by the metes and bounds aforesaid. And that all the rest of the villages within the hundred of Ongar aforesaid in the same twentieth year above said, were and remained entirely out of the forest aforesaid. And that all the half hundred of Waltham aforesaid, in the twentieth year of the said late King James of England, &c., with all the lands, woods, and hereditaments in the several villages within the half hundred, entirely remained within the forest aforesaid, unless the lands of any person or persons lying within the half hundred aforesaid are disafforested by any charter, which they made not to appear to the jurors aforesaid. And that in the same twentieth year of the late King James of England, &c., the whole half hundred of Harlow aforesaid, and the hundred of Uttlesford, Hinkford, Lexden, Tendring, Dengi, Witham, Chelmsford, Dunmow, Clavering,

Freshwell, Chafford, Barstaple, Thurstable, Rochford, and Winstree, in the aforesaid county of Essex, and all the villages and parishes with all and singular their members, and appendages, and each of them, with all lands, meadow pastures, woods, tenements, and hereditaments whatsoever within the villages and parishes of the hundreds last mentioned, remained entirely out of the forest aforesaid.

And the jurors aforesaid further upon their oaths aforesaid, say that in the said twentieth year of the reign of King James aforesaid, and before, as it is before said, within the memory of men, they find not, nor can find, any other or more forest, or forests, to be within the county of Essex, except the forest aforesaid, in manner as before limited and bounded.

In witness whereof, as well the Commissioners aforesaid and jurors aforesaid, subscribe and set their hands and seals to these presents.

THOMAS BENDISH.
BENJAMIN AYLOFFE.
WILLIAM ROW.
HEN. HOLCROFTE.
WM. MARTYN.
WM. CONYERS.
THOMAS FANSHAW.
EDWARD KEIGLEY (Verderer).
CAREW HARVEY, otherwise MILDMAY (Verderer)
EDW. PALMER (Verderer).
JOHN WRIGHT.
WILLIAM ATWOOD.'

The first person named in this inquisition, as being summoned under the sheriff's writ, appears to be Thomas Manwood, Gent. He was the writer or compiler of the book known by the name of *Manwood's Forest Laws*, to which we are now wholly indebted for all we have relative to the forest laws, and forest administration as truly authentic, since all the forest records have been smugged.

The compiler has before heard of boys smugging other boys marbles, but never heard of men smugging the records of a public court of English judicature before.

Publications List

Transactions No 1 1970*: ISBN 9028 9300 9, £1

Transactions No 2 1974: ISBN 9028 9300 7, £1

Pohl, D J: *Loughton 1851 – the Village and its People* 1988*: ISBN 9028 9302 5, £3

Elliott, B: *History of the Loughton and Chigwell Police* 1991: ISBN 9028 9303 3, £2

Russell, V J and Dare, E H: *A Walk Round Chigwell* 1992, 75p

Ambrose, P: *Reminiscences of a Loughton Life* 1995*: ISBN 0952 53440 1, £5.25

Paar, H W: *Loughton's First Railway Station* 1996*: ISBN 0952 88050 4, £3.50

Hunter, R, Elliot, W H and Pond, C C: *The Life of Robert Hunter 1823–1897, Lexicographer, Missionary, Geologist and Naturalist* 1997*: ISBN 0952 88051 2, £5

Pond, C C: *History of the Loughton Methodist Church and of Methodist Expansion in SW Essex* 1998: ISBN 0952 88052 0, £4

Whiting, A: *The Loughton Roding Estate, From Cattle-Grazing to Double-Glazing* 1998: ISBN 0952 88053 9, £3

Wilkinson, D: *From Mean Streets to Epping Forest: The Shaftesbury Retreat, Loughton* 2000: ISBN 0952 88054 7, £3

Waller, W C [Pond, C C, Ed]: *Notes on Loughton 1890-95* 2001: ISBN 0952 88056 3, £1.50

Morris, R S: *William Chapman Waller 1850-1917: Loughton's Historian* (hardbound book with 16 pages of colour plates) (2001)*: ISBN 0952 88055 5, £7.50

Morris, R S and Pond, C C Eds*: *Loughton a Hundred Years Ago* 2001: ISBN 0952 88057 1, £5.50

Pond, C C: *A Walk Round Loughton* 2005, £1.25

Waller, W C [Morris, R S, Ed]: *Notes on Loughton – II: 1896-1914* 2002: ISBN 0952 88059 8, £2.00

Lockington, E and Trickey, W: *The Coffee House at Woodford* 2002: ISBN 0954 2314 1 4, £5

Pond, C and C: *Walks in Loughton's Forest* 2002: ISBN 0954 2314 0 6, £3

Woodhouse, Peter: *Life in Loughton 1926–46* 2003: ISBN 0954 2314 5 7, £5

Pond, C C: *The Buildings of Loughton and Notable People of the Town* 2003: ISBN 0954 2314 3 0, £5

Morris, R S: *The Powells in Essex and their London Ancestors* (hardbound book with 16 pages of colour plates) (2003): ISBN 0954 2314 2 2, £9.50

Morris, R S: *The Verderers and Courts of Waltham Forest in the County of Essex 1250–2000* (hardbound book with 16 pages of colour plates) (2004): ISBN 0954 2314 6 5, £14.95

Green, Gertrude [Pond, C C, Ed]: *My Life in Loughton* 2004: ISBN 0954 2314 7 3, £5

Morris, R S: *The Harveys of Rolls Park, Chigwell, Essex* 2005: ISBN 0954 2314 9 X, £5

Taylor, Sue: *Lady Mary Wroth* 2005: ISBN 0954 2314 81, £2.50

Morris, R S Ed: *Maynard's Concise History of Epping Forest 1860* 2005: ISBN 1905 2960 13, £3

Books are softbound except those indicated as hardbound, above. Titles marked * are out-of-print, or only a few copies are left in stock. Items can be had by post (cash with order – cheques payable to Loughton and District Historical Society) from Forest Villa, Staples Road, Loughton, Essex, IG10 1HP at the prices given – post free in the UK, cash with order. For post abroad, with payment in dollars or other currencies, please write or e-mail Loughton_Ponds@hotmail.com first. Overseas postage charged at cost.

10 per cent discount on direct sales to schools, libraries and record offices. Books sent on invoice after official order.